SOME MAJOR EVENTS IN WORLD WAR II

THE EUROPEAN THEATER

1939 SEPTEMBER—Germany invades Poland; Great Britain, France, Australia, & New Zealand declare war on Germany; Battle of the Atlantic begins. NOVEMBER—Russia invades Finland.

1940 APRIL—Germany invades Denmark & Norway. MAY—Germany invades Belgium, Luxembourg, & The Netherlands; British forces retreat to Dunkirk and escape to England. JUNE—Italy declares war on Britain & France; France surrenders to Germany. JULY—Battle of Britain begins. SEPTEMBER—Italy invades Egypt; Germany, Italy, & Japan form the Axis countries. OCTOBER—Italy invades Greece. NOVEMBER—Battle of Britain over. DECEMBER—Britain attacks Italy in North Africa.

1941 JANUARY—Allies take Tobruk. FEBRUARY—Rommel arrives at Tripoli. APRIL—Germany invades Greece & Yugoslavia. JUNE—Allies are in Syria; Germany invades Russia. JULY—Russia joins Allies. AUGUST—Germans capture Kiev. OCTOBER—Germany reaches Moscow. DECEMBER—Germans retreat from Moscow; Japan attacks Pearl Harbor; United States enters war against Axis nations.

1942 MAY—first British bomber attack on Cologne. JUNE—Germans take Tobruk. SEPTEMBER—Battle of Stalingrad begins. OCTOBER—Battle of El Alamein begins. NOVEMBER—Allies recapture Tobruk; Russians counterattack at Stalingrad.

1943 JANUARY—Allies take Tripoli. FEBRUARY—German troops at Stalingrad surrender. APRIL—revolt of Warsaw Ghetto Jews begins. MAY—German and Italian resistance in North Africa is over; their troops surrender in Tunisia; Warsaw Ghetto revolt is put down by Germany. JULY—allies invade Sicily; Mussolini put in prison. SEPTEMBER—Allies land in Italy; Italians surrender; Germans occupy Rome; Mussolini rescued by Germany. OCTOBER—Allies capture Naples; Italy declares war on Germany. NOVEMBER—Russians recapture Kiev.

1944 JANUARY—Allies land at Anzio. JUNE—Rome falls to Allies; Allies land in Normandy (D-Day). JULY—assassination attempt on Hitler fails. AUGUST—Allies land in southern France. SEPTEMBER—Brussels freed. OCTOBER—Athens liberated. DECEMBER—Battle of the Bulge.

1945 JANUARY—Russians free Warsaw. FEBRUARY—Dresden bombed. APRIL—Americans take Belsen and Buchenwald concentration camps; Russians free Vienna; Russians take over Berlin; Mussolini killed; Hitler commits suicide. MAY—Germany surrenders; Goering captured.

THE PACIFIC THEATER

1940 SEPTEMBER—Japan joins Axis nations Germany & Italy.

1941 APRIL—Russia & Japan sign neutrality pact. DECEMBER—Japanese launch attacks against Pearl Harbor, Hong Kong, the Philippines, & Malaya; United States and Allied nations declare war on Japan; China declares war on Japan, Germany, & Italy; Japan takes over Guam, Wake Island, & Hong Kong; Japan attacks Burma.

1942 JANUARY—Japan takes over Manila; Japan invades Dutch East Indies. FEBRUARY—Japan takes over Singapore; Battle of the Java Sea. APRIL—Japanese overrun Bataan. MAY—Japan takes Mandalay; Allied forces in Philippines surrender to Japan; Japan takes Corregidor; Battle of the Coral Sea. JUNE—Battle of Midway; Japan occupies Aleutian Islands. AUGUST—United States invades Guadalcanal in the Solomon Islands.

1943 FEBRUARY—Guadalcanal taken by U.S. Marines. MARCH—Japanese begin to retreat in China. APRIL—Yamamoto shot down by U.S. Air Force. MAY—U.S. troops take Aleutian Islands back from Japan. JUNE—Allied troops land in New Guinea. NOVEMBER—U.S. Marines invade Bougainville & Tarawa.

1944 FEBRUARY—Truk liberated. JUNE—Saipan attacked by United States. JULY—battle for Guam begins. OCTOBER—U.S. troops invade Philippines; Battle of Leyte Gulf won by Allies.

1945 JANUARY—Luzon taken; Burma Road won back. MARCH—Iwo Jima freed. APRIL—Okinawa attacked by U.S. troops; President Franklin Roosevelt dies; Harry S. Truman becomes president. JUNE—United States takes Okinawa. AUGUST—atomic bomb dropped on Hiroshima; Russia declares war on Japan; atomic bomb dropped on Nagasaki. SEPTEMBER—Japan surrenders.

WORLD AT WAR

Goering and
the Luftwaffe

WORLD AT WAR

Goering and the Luftwaffe

By G.C. Skipper

CHILDRENS PRESS, CHICAGO

EUROPE 1939

FRONTISPIECE:

Adolf Hitler (middle) with an aide and Reichminister of Aviation General Hermann Goering (right). They had met to review air maneuvers by the Richtofen Squadron of the Luftwaffe.

Library of Congress Cataloging in Publication Data

Skipper, G.C.
 Goering and the Luftwaffe.
 (His World at war)
 SUMMARY: An account of Hermann Goering's role in Nazi Germany, in the creation of the Luftwaffe, and in World War II.
 1. Göring, Hermann, 1893-1946—Juvenile literature.
2. Germany. Luftwaffe—History—Juvenile literature.
3. Statesmen—Germany—Biography—Juvenile literature.
4. Marshals—Germany—Biography—Juvenile literature.
[1. Göring, Hermann, 1893-1946. 2. Statesmen.
3. World War, 1939-1945—Germany] I. Title. II. Series.
DD247.G67S55 943.086'092'4 [B] [92] 80-16947
ISBN 0-516-04784-1

Ch. Pres. 3.24.81 - 5-85 6-06

PICTURE CREDITS:

NATIONAL ARCHIVES: Cover, pages 15, 19, 2 32

UPI: pages 4, 10 (bottom), 12, 13, 14, 17, 24, 28, 31, 35, 44 (bottom), 45

U.S. ARMY PHOTOGRAPH: pages 9, 10 (top), 39, 40, 41, 42, 45 (top)

U.S. AIR FORCE PHOTO: pages 21, 34, 36

LEN MEENTS (maps): pages 6, 9, 31, 32

COVER PHOTO:

Hermann Goering addressing the Reichst

At first the sound that came from the sky was distant, undefined. Certainly it was not thunder. The Polish airmen stopped what they were doing and listened. The faraway sound settled into a faint roar.

"What in the world is that?" asked one of the airmen.

His companion was polishing a pair of boots. He didn't answer. He stopped whisking the brush across his boots. He frowned, listening.

The sound grew louder and louder. Suddenly the puzzlement on the faces of the airmen turned to terror.

"Germans!" one of them shouted. He threw down the brush. "The Nazis are attacking!"

As he spoke, alarms went off all over the base. Everyone was alerted to the approaching danger. The airmen scrambled outside. They ran toward the airplanes waiting on the airstrip.

The roar of the Nazi engines grew into a howl of noise. Suddenly, through the noise, came the scream and whistle of bombs.

"Watch out!" someone cried.

But even as the words were uttered, the bombs hit. They came down in a horrifying hail of disaster. The bombs exploded. They blasted away the barracks. The explosions killed hundreds of Polish pilots. The bombs destroyed much of the Polish air force as it sat on the ground.

Those Polish planes that did manage to take off ran into the full might and power of the deadly Luftwaffe—the Nazi air force.

It was September 1, 1939. Within a month, Nazi Germany had crushed the Polish defenses.

The capital of Poland is Warsaw. On October 5, 1939, Adolf Hitler paraded in triumph through the Warsaw streets. The entire world was stunned and shocked.

The short, brutal victory of the Germans was due to the *blitzkrieg*. It was a method which, at that time, the world had never seen.

The Luftwaffe swarmed in and destroyed the air defense. On the heels of the Luftwaffe came

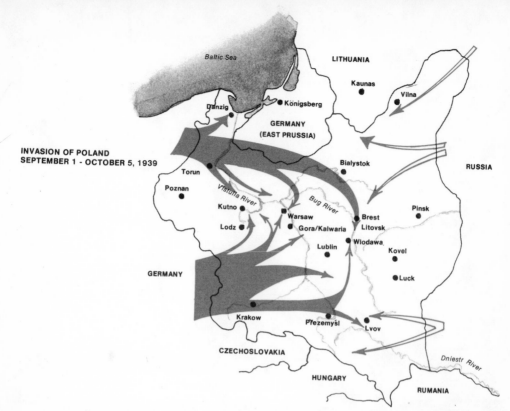

INVASION OF POLAND
SEPTEMBER 1 - OCTOBER 5, 1939

Members of the German High Command watch German soldiers cross into Poland on September 1, 1939.

Goering was delighted with the success of the Nazi invasion of Poland.

the ground troops. Armored panzer (tank) divisions and infantry troops charged through the lines of defense. For the first time the world learned the word blitzkrieg. The world also learned to fear that word. It means "lightning war."

Among the Nazis who were delighted with the victory on that day in early October was a fat, jovial man. His soft, pampered flesh seemed more fitting for a woman than a military man. Other than Hitler himself, this man was the most familiar and prominent figure in Nazi Germany.

His name was also known throughout the world. He was known for his intelligence, his enormous energy, his charm, and his sense of humor. He had read widely. He had expert knowledge of paintings, rare books, sculpture, and other works of art.

The man was Hermann Wilhelm Goering. He had grown fantastically wealthy during the past four years. He owned several mansions. One of

When Goering married his second wife, actress Emmy Sonnemann, his uniform was covered with dazzling medals. Hitler was best man at the marriage ceremony and attended the wedding feast.

The Goerings with their baby daughter, Edda, on Goering's forty-sixth birthday in January, 1939.

them was named Karinhall, for his first wife who had died. Goering now had a second wife. He also had a small child.

Because of his new family, he wasn't really anxious to see Germany at war. That could mean the loss of his mansions, his wealth, and even his family.

Yet it became obvious that Hitler would start a war. Goering threw every ounce of his energy and intelligence into backing *Der Fuehrer* (the leader).

This picture, taken for propaganda purposes, shows Goering reading a special edition of Adolf Hitler's book, *Mein Kampf.*

Goering grew up as an aristocrat. He lived in castles that were owned by other people. Now he owned his own castles and grand estates. He had become wealthy by taking money that belonged to the state. Also, the Nazis were so feared by 1939 that many wealthy businessmen freely gave expensive gifts and money for favors. Much of that money and many of the gifts went to Hermann Goering. He was the second most important man in the Third Reich.

World War I air ace Goering in one of the planes he flew.

Goering believed he deserved his wealth. After all, in World War I he had been an ace fighter pilot. Germany, however, lost World War I. The country was cut off from the rest of Europe. Germany suffered in the humiliation of defeat. Germany's economy suffered from inflation and unemployment.

It was during this time that Goering met Adolf Hitler. Like many others, he followed Hitler. Goering was with Hitler in 1923. In the city of Munich that year, Hitler's National Socialist Party tried to take over the government at pistol point.

That attempt failed miserably. Street fighting broke out. The police fired on Hitler's storm troopers. Goering was at Hitler's side. He was shot during the brief battle and fell to the street.

When the fighting ended, Hitler was sent to jail. Goering was suffering from the gunshot wound. He was hustled out of Germany to Italy. Later he was sneaked into Switzerland.

By the time Goering reached Switzerland he was suffering badly. Finally, he received medical attention. To ease Goering's pain, the doctors prescribed two shots of morphine every day.

It did not take long for Goering to become a drug addict. After his wounds healed, he continued to take morphine. While Hitler was serving his time in jail, Goering was living in Switzerland. His drug habit was growing worse.

His morphine addiction became so bad that he became dangerous. Finally he was certified as a dangerous drug addict. He was placed in a hospital for treatment.

After he was released from the hospital, things changed for the better. Goering was allowed to return to Germany in 1927. He renewed his efforts for the Nazi Party. Hitler had learned one thing well. He could not take the government with a pistol. He decided to take control through legal means—by vote.

By 1933 Hitler had reached his goal. He was named chancellor (prime minister) of Germany. He soon became a dictator. He called the government the Third Reich. Because of Goering's loyalty, Hitler promptly named Goering Minister Without Portfolio. Goering loved long, fancy titles. By 1936 he had become President of the Reichstag. This was Germany's governing body, or parliament.

The first meeting of the new Nazi cabinet, headed by Adolf Hitler as chancellor, was held in February, 1933. Seated next to Hitler are Goering (left) and Vice Chancellor Von Papen (right).

By 1939, when the Nazis crushed Poland, Goering had many other titles. And he had all the power that went with them. He was Prussian Premier and Minister of the Interior. He was also Reichminister of Aviation. It was in this position that he built the Luftwaffe into one of the most fearsome air-attack units in the world.

Goering, who recently had been appointed Reichminister of Aviation and the German Economic Coordinator, makes a speech in November, 1936.

To hide Germany's military buildup, the Air Ministry was created. The world did not know Germany had an air force until it was too late. By then the Luftwaffe was a deadly, powerful force. Nothing—or so it seemed—could stop it.

In addition to all his other titles, Goering also was economic dictator of the Reich. Hitler gave him that powerful position in 1936. And why not? After all, Goering had built the mighty Luftwaffe from almost nothing.

Before its rise to power, the Nazi party had only a handful of airplanes. These had been used to shuttle speakers to and from political rallies. Hermann Goering's ability as an organizer was unquestioned.

Hitler's plane on the way to a rally. A small number of these shuttle planes formed the base on which the mighty Luftwaffe was built.

In 1939 the Nazi High Command listened to the chorus of cheers from the soldiers in Warsaw. "Heil, Hitler's!" echoed throughout the streets.

Goering felt a great sense of pride as he stood there in Warsaw that day. The world saw his jovial face. People would learn of his charm, wit, and intelligence. It was hard to believe that this man was evil.

But the world did not truly know Hermann Goering. Only later was it to learn that Hermann Goering was the man who created the Gestapo, the Nazi secret police that spread torture, fear, and death. It was Hermann Goering who planned the economic strategy that ruined the Jews in Germany. It was also Hermann Goering who laid out the plans for the starvation of millions of Russian citizens if, and when, Germany defeated Russia.

While doing all these things, Goering still had time to create the Luftwaffe—which he was extremely proud of. The Luftwaffe was designed for short-range operations. Goering believed, as did Hitler, that the Luftwaffe could be master of the skies. All it needed was medium-range bombers, dive-bombers such as the Junkers 87, and fighters, such as the Messerschmitt 109.

Goering believed there was no need for heavy, long-range bombers. With the short-range, quick-hit type of air fighting, wars could be won fast and at little expense.

These German fighter planes, Messerschmitt 109s, were an important part of the Luftwaffe.

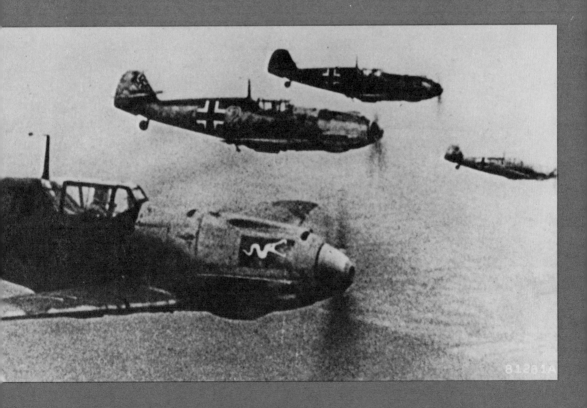

In September, 1938, exactly one year before the invasion of Poland, Hitler greets Goering at a Nazi Party rally.

But Goering was wrong in his belief, as was Hitler. The Luftwaffe also had other flaws. The intelligence units were often wrong. The information they gave Goering was incorrect. Goering and Hitler, however, had no reason to believe their Luftwaffe policy was flawed. To prove this they pointed to the successful record of the Luftwaffe.

After all, the defeat of Poland had taken only three weeks—thanks to Goering's air force.

"Leave it to my Luftwaffe," Goering would say, laughing.

The success of the Luftwaffe convinced Goering and Hitler that any nation could be defeated if the Nazis used bombers. Total faith in bombing techniques, however, was the very factor that eventually destroyed the Luftwaffe.

Things were rolling along well on the military front. But things were not going so well with Goering. His relationship with Hitler had begun to sour. Goering and Hitler argued on several occasions—especially about the methods that would be used to take Czechoslovakia. Goering wanted to do it through economic pressure. Hitler wanted to use military force.

Hitler did not like Goering's attitude. Besides, Goering was becoming something of an embarrassment. Rumors circulated about his drug addiction. Hitler could live with that. But other things bothered many of the Nazis.

They felt that a man of Goering's position and power should have great dignity. Instead, Goering often embarrassed those who visited him at his mansion, Karinhall. Goering would greet them wearing outlandish costumes. One resembled a

Goering, appointed Chief German Huntsman, poses in a new
uniform befitting the post. Jokes about Goering's
fantastic uniforms constantly made the rounds in Germany.

Robin Hood outfit. He wore this when conducting
tours around the estate. Goering would rush back
to Karinhall ahead of the other guests. When they
arrived, he would reappear to greet them wearing
a garish silk gown with puffed sleeves. He wore
numerous diamond rings and often wore a golden
dagger stuck in his belt.

Goering was extremely vain. Nothing pleased him more than to take visitors up to the attic in Karinhall. There he would show them his large collection of electric trains. He would sit in an armchair and run the toy trains. He had built an elaborate system. Tiny airplanes would come down and drop toy bombs on the trains as they ran the length of the room.

This strange behavior was caused, no doubt, by Goering's drug addiction. As Goering began to neglect some of his duties, Hitler found it necessary to get more competent people to handle the affairs. However, not until the very end did Hitler relieve Goering of his positions and power.

Once Hitler sent a Nazi named Schellenberg out to see Goering at Karinhall. When Schellenberg arrived, he was ushered into the enormous mansion.

"The reich marshal will be with you shortly," said the servant, and went away.

Schellenberg waited and waited. No one appeared. He continued to wait. He knew he could not return to Hitler until he had met with Goering.

Nearly two hours passed. Finally, Goering came bounding into the room. He held out his hand to greet his visitor. Schellenberg was shocked—for Goering was wearing a Roman toga and sandals.

On another occasion Goering showed up at the dining table dressed in a long flowing silk gown and house slippers.

Another time he tried to direct a Luftwaffe attack from Karinhall. He sent the airplanes in the wrong direction.

These stories were popping around Hitler's ears like firecrackers. Still Hitler would not get rid of the fat man who had been loyal to the party for so long.

Hitler and Goering's relationship improved when the Luftwaffe played such a successful role in taking Poland. By 1939, the relationship was still fairly solid. Hitler even announced publicly that Goering would be his successor as leader of the Third Reich—should there ever be need for a successor.

Goering inspecting his troops

Newly appointed a field marshal, Goering shows off his baton as he reviews troops on the third anniversary of the official creation of the Luftwaffe.

Everyone was stunned at this—except Hermann Goering. He had been saying for years that he would take Hitler's place—if something should happen to Hitler.

So Goering felt very good about the development of his personal career in late 1939. At that time Hitler called a conference to announce that he was planning to attack the West. The way to accomplish this, said Hitler, was by using the Luftwaffe. Goering beamed. The invasion of Britain was also discussed. Goering was entirely convinced that the Luftwaffe alone could beat Britain. He did not need the help of the army or the navy.

There was much arguing among the military leaders, but when things settled down, it had been decided. The Luftwaffe would play a key role in the attack on the West.

The attack date, said Hitler, would be in early 1940.

Then things went terribly wrong. Nazi Major Helmut Reinberger, a staff officer of the

Luftwaffe, was flying to a conference. He got lost and had to make a forced landing in Belgium. Major Reinberger was carrying the entire plan of attack.

Hitler had no choice. He delayed the attack date. Another conference was called on January 13, 1940, to decide what to do. Attending were Goering, Hitler, and another top official named Keitel. Although Hitler was calm about the incident, Goering raged. He pounded the table. He was furious that a staff officer of "his Luftwaffe" could make such a blundering mistake.

After all the shouting, the conference got down to business. Hitler decided to attack the West in the spring. He would attack Norway and Denmark first. Goering's Luftwaffe would be a key factor in the attack.

Again, the Nazis hit fast and unexpectedly. Denmark fell under the onslaught without a fight. Norway, however, fought back. The Luftwaffe

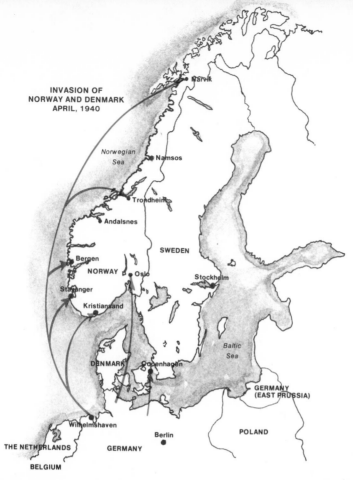

INVASION OF
NORWAY AND DENMARK
APRIL, 1940

At one of the many conferences held to plan the attack on the West, Goering, Keitel, and Hitler (left to right) plot strategy.

31

THE NETHERLANDS (HOLLAND)

INVASION OF HOLLAND, BELGIUM, LUXEMBOURG, AND FRANCE MAY-JUNE, 1940

Hamburg

Groningen

Oldenburg

Amsterdam

Deventer Enschede

The Hague   Utrecht

Rotterdam   Lok R.

Rhine R.

Arnheim

Maas R.

Breda

Düsseldorf

Ostend   Antwerp

GERMANY

Dunkirk   Albert Canal   Louvhin

BELGIUM   Brussels   Ft. Eban Emael

Somme R.   Liege

Arras   Somme R.

Somme R.   **FRANCE**   **LUX.**

Amiens   Luxembourg

Rouen   Aisne R.   Meuse R.

Seine R.   Oise R.   Reims

Marne R.

Paris

Rhine R.

The German army fighting in the mountains of Norway

zoomed in and blasted Sola Airfield. It didn't take long for the Nazis to take it.

But the king of Norway had no intention of yielding to the Nazi force. He fled with his government to a tiny village. Goering sent the Luftwaffe after him. The mighty Nazi air force went in to bomb the village. They ran smack into fierce resistance. The Luftwaffe didn't do very well.

To make matters worse, the Nazi navy suffered severe damages and losses, which hurt Hitler's plans badly.

For a while Goering was afraid he would lose favor with Hitler again. But, surprisingly, he didn't. Hitler, instead, turned his attack plans on Holland and Belgium. By this time the Luftwaffe had grown into the largest air force in the world.

The attack was launched. Holland, Belgium, and France were defeated in less than six weeks. This surprised even the Nazis themselves. One of the key factors that led to the success was the Luftwaffe operation. Goering's airborne troops parachuted into Holland. They took the Dutch totally by surprise.

German bombers on a mission in England

Goering's bombers did the rest. They blasted away at Rotterdam without mercy, even while the Dutch were trying to negotiate a peace settlement.

Finally came the time to attack Britain. Goering's Luftwaffe had already failed to stop the evacuation at Dunkirk. From there, 338,000 British, French, Belgian, and Dutch troops had been picked up and moved across the English Channel to England.

Again, Hitler did not rage and scream about Goering's failure.

On August 2, 1940, Goering told his Luftwaffe, "Destroy the Royal Air Force of Britain."

Goering in the pilot's cabin of a Nazi bomber during a visit to one of his air squadrons.

As the Russians moved relentlessly toward Berlin in May, 1945, the Nazi exodus began in earnest. No German wanted to be captured by the feared Russians. Hundreds of Nazis fled toward the more gentle American forces to surrender. Goèring himself fled Berlin.

He sat back and waited to bask in another glorious victory. That was the beginning of the Battle of Britain. When the Luftwaffe tried to bring Britain to her knees it met its match.

The whole operation proved disastrous for the Luftwaffe. For all practical purposes the once mighty Nazi air force would never be the same again.

Hitler acknowledged Goering's failure when he called off the invasion of Britain.

The entire war began to turn. The Nazis were defeated on all fronts. By 1945 the Nazis had lost the war. Hitler huddled in his Berlin bunker and planned his own death. He ordered Hermann Goering to leave the bunker to handle matters outside Berlin.

Goering was more than glad to go. He crated up all the paintings and art treasures he had bought and stolen and moved out quickly. Knowing Hitler's determination to stay and die in Berlin, Goering sent a message to Hitler asking if it was time for him to take over the government. He was, after all, Hitler's successor.

Hitler was furious. He accused Goering of high treason. He stripped him of all his titles, his offices, and his power. The only reason Hitler did not have Goering killed was that Goering had been loyal to the party.

After Hitler killed himself in the bunker, Goering was among the masses of Nazis trying to escape from the oncoming Russians.

On May 5, 1945, Hermann Goering was captured by the United States Army.

When the war ended, the world learned of the atrocities committed by the Nazis in the concentration and extermination camps. The International Military Tribunal was created to try the Nazis for war crimes.

Hermann Goering was the most prominent Nazi to be tried at Nuremberg.

While being held prisoner, waiting for the Nuremburg trials to begin, doctors helped Goering

Left: During a press interview after his capture in May, 1945, Goering told reporters how he was placed under arrest by Hitler and then was rescued by his Luftwaffe men.

Below: Goering removes his medals during processing after his capture.

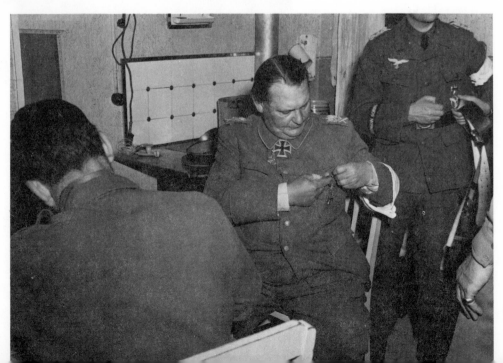

Films showing scenes like this one, taken at the liberation of the Buchenwald concentration camp, made most of the Nazis weep during the Nuremberg trials. Goering, however, showed no emotion.

rid himself of his drug addiction. Goering's enormous weight went down and he regained his brilliance.

Goering basked in the glory of being the top Nazi on trial. He argued his defense so well that even the trial judges were amazed at the man.

"I only thought we would eliminate Jews from positions in big business and government, and that was that," Goering said.

But when the films of the concentration and death camps were shown during the trial, the other Nazis broke down and wept with shame.

Left: Goering eating
breakfast in Cell Number
before the trials began.

Below: The first
session of the
Nuremburg trials.

Goering on the stand at Nuremburg

Goering stared at the floor. But he continued to be faithful to Hitler. He defended him and his actions. Goering proudly bore his share of the responsibility for murdering millions of men, women, and children.

At the end of the trial, Goering was found guilty. The prosecution said, "His guilt is unique in its enormity. The record discloses no excuses for this man."

When sentence was passed, the International Military Tribunal said, "Hermann Wilhelm Goering, on the counts of the indictment on which you have been convicted, the International Military Tribunal sentences you to death by hanging."

Goering stood in the dock with earphones clamped to his head to hear the translation. He heard his death sentence. He dropped the earphones, turned, and walked out.

When he returned to his cell, Goering was pale. He began trembling. He picked up a book, but it didn't help.

The next morning, however, he had regained his composure. He petitioned the court to let him die like a soldier—before a firing squad. Goering's request was refused.

Goering was to lead the other convicted Nazis to the gallows on October 15, 1945. He was scheduled to be the first to hang.

But, somehow, Goering had managed to sneak into Cell 5 a vial of poison. Rather than face the gallows, shortly less than two hours before he was to hang, Hermann Goering took the poison. His death was slow and painful. The guards found him on the floor of his cell, but they couldn't save him.

The executions of the Nazis were not interrupted by Goering's suicide. Another convicted Nazi named Ribbentrop took Goering's place and led the others to the gallows. Ribbentrop was hanged first.

Then came the others—Keitel, Kaltenbrunner, Rosenberg, Frank, Frick, Streicher, Sauckel, Jodl, and Seyss-Inquart.

After the Nazis were hanged, their bodies were burned.

The body of Hermann Goering was removed from Cell 5 and burned with the others.

Below: Goering's wife and daughter look down from a photo at part of his fabulous secret treasure hoard. His great wealth during the war was a stark contrast to the meager worldly possessions he had in his cell at the end of his life (above).

About the Author

A native of Alabama, G.C. Skipper has traveled throughout the world, including Jamaica, Haiti, India, Argentina, the Bahamas, and Mexico. He has written several other children's books as well as an adult novel. Mr. Skipper has also published numerous articles in national magazines. He is now working on his second adult novel. Mr. Skipper and his family live in Norristown, Pennsylvania, a suburb of Philadelphia.